# SOUND INNOVATIONS

## ENSEMBLE DEVELOPMENT

### Chorales and Warm-up Exercises for Tone, Technique and Rhythm

## YOUNG CONCERT BAND

Peter **BOONSHAFT** | Chris **BERNOTAS**

Thank you for making *Sound Innovations Ensemble Development for Young Concert Band* a part of your large ensemble curriculum. With 167 exercises, including more than 100 chorales by some of today's most renowned young band composers, this book will be a valuable resource in helping you grow in your understanding and abilities as an ensemble musician.

An assortment of exercises, grouped by key, are presented in a variety of young band difficulty levels. Where possible, several exercises in the same category are provided to allow variety while accomplishing the goals of that specific type of exercise. You will notice that many exercises and chorales are clearly marked with dynamics, articulations, style and tempo for you to practice those aspects of performance. Other exercises are intentionally left for you or your teacher to determine how best to use them in reaching your performance goals.

Whether you are progressing through exercises to better your technical facility or challenging your musicianship with beautiful chorales, we are confident you will be excited, motivated and inspired by using *Sound Innovations Ensemble Development for Young Concert Band*.

© 2016 Alfred Music
Sound Innovations® is a registered trademark of Alfred Music
All Rights Reserved including Public Performance

ISBN-10: 1-4706-3400-7
ISBN-13: 978-1-4706-3400-1

Instrument photos courtesy of Yamaha Corporation of America Band & Orchestral Division

2

# Concert B♭ Major

**1  LONG TONES**

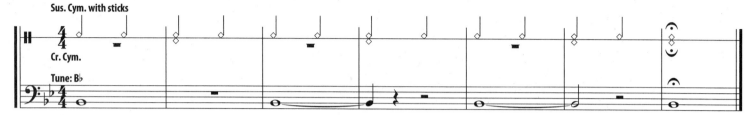

**2  PASSING THE TONIC**

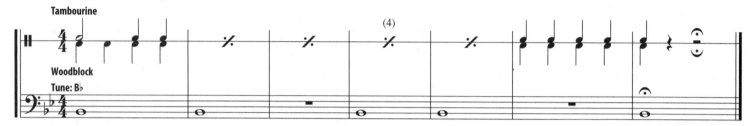

**3  PASSING THE TONIC**

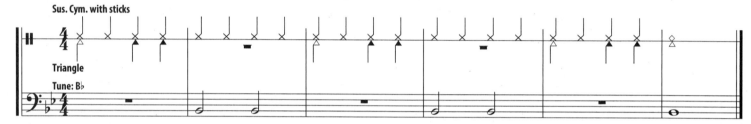

**4  PITCH MATCHING: WOODWIND MOUTHPIECES WITH BAND ACCOMPANIMENT**

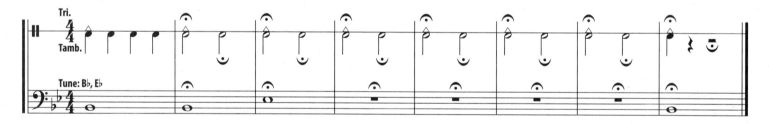

**5  SCALE BUILDER**

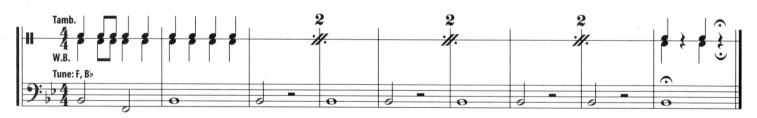

**6  SCALE BUILDER**

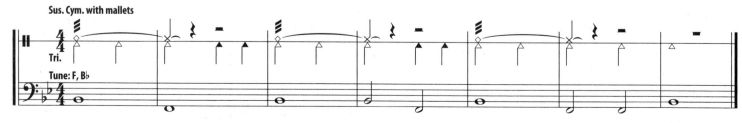

**7 EXPANDING INTERVALS: DIATONIC**

**8 EXPANDING INTERVALS: CHROMATIC**

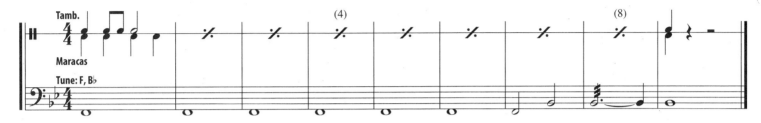

**9 INTERVAL BUILDER: DIATONIC INTERVALS**

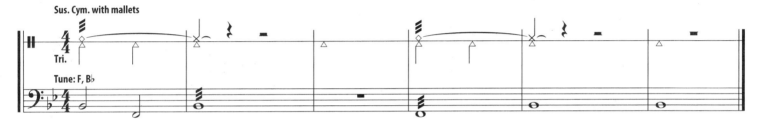

**10 INTERVAL BUILDER: PERFECT INTERVALS**

**11 CHORD BUILDER**

**12 CHORD BUILDER**

**13 MOVING CHORD TONES**

4

## 14 DIATONIC HARMONY

## 15 DIATONIC HARMONY

## 16 RHYTHMIC SOUNDS

Play the repeated section at least 4 times.

## 17 RHYTHMIC SUBDIVISION

## 18 5-NOTE SCALE

## 19 CANON: 5-NOTE SCALE

## 20 CANON: 6-NOTE SCALE

5

1 **CANON: 8-NOTE SCALE**

**22 CHORALE: 5-NOTE SCALE**

Chris M. Bernotas (ASCAP)

**23 CHORALE: 5-NOTE SCALE**

Chris M. Bernotas (ASCAP)

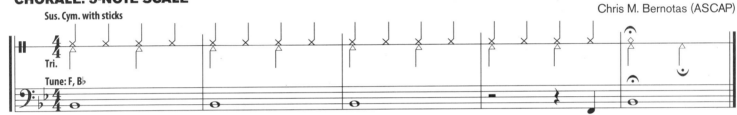

**24 CHORALE: 6-NOTE SCALE**

Chris M. Bernotas (ASCAP)

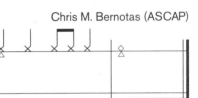
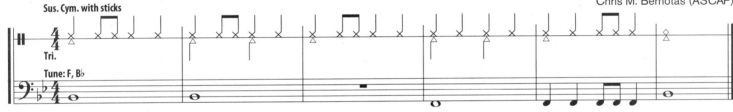

**25 CHORALE: 8-NOTE SCALE**

Chris M. Bernotas (ASCAP)

**26 CHORALE: 8-NOTE SCALE**

Chris M. Bernotas (ASCAP)

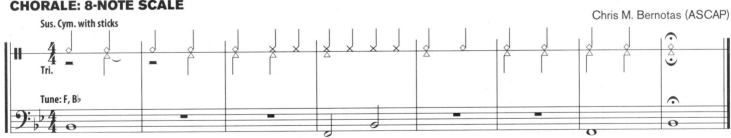

**27 CHORALE**

Robert Sheldon (ASCAP)

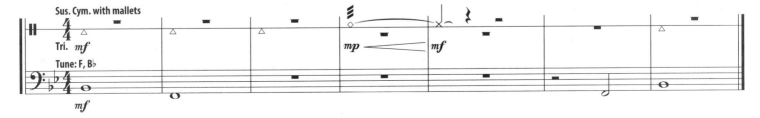

6

## 28 CHORALE

Moderato

John O'Reilly (ASCAP)

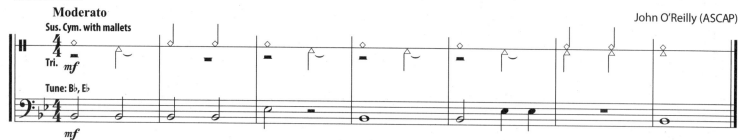

## 29 CHORALE

Ralph Ford (ASCAP)

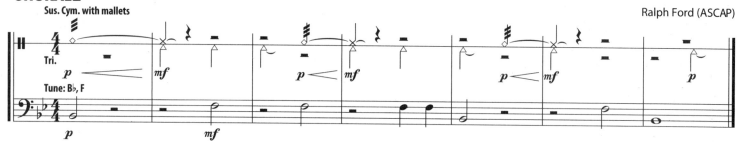

## 30 CHORALE

Moderately

Michael Story (ASCAP)

## 31 CHORALE

Randall D. Standridge (ASCAP)

## 32 CHORALE

Roland Barrett (ASCAP)

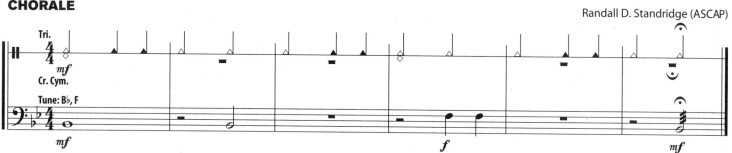

## 33 CHORALE

Slowly

Chris M. Bernotas (ASCAP)

**34** **CHORALE**

Rob Grice (ASCAP)

**35** **CHORALE**

Matt Conaway (ASCAP)

**Very smoothly**

**36** **CHORALE**

Scott Watson (BMI)

**Largo**

**37** **CHORALE**

Todd Stalter (ASCAP)

**Maestoso**

**38** **CHORALE**

Robert Sheldon (ASCAP)

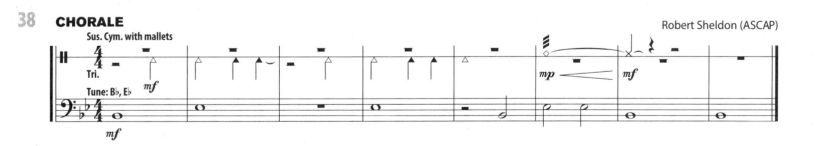

**39** **CHORALE**

Tyler S. Grant (ASCAP)

**Moderately**

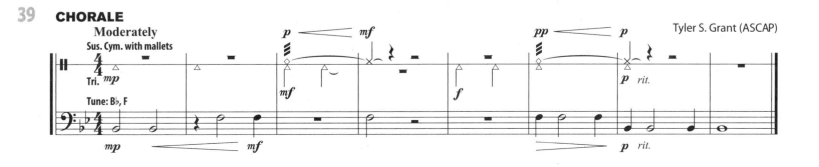

8

**40 CHORALE**

Randall D. Standridge (ASCAP)

**41 CHORALE**

Maestoso

Todd Stalter (ASCAP)

**42 CHORALE**

Moderately slow

Michael Story (ASCAP)

**43 CHORALE**

Ralph Ford (ASCAP)

**44 CHORALE**

Andante

John O'Reilly (ASCAP)

**45 CHORALE**

"Finally the first smells of Summer were in the air. 'Time to plant those strange seeds we found,' she thought."

Jodie Blackshaw (ASCAP)

**46  CHORALE**

Matt Conaway (ASCAP)

Gently flowing

**47  CHORALE**

Randall D. Standridge (ASCAP)

**48  CHORALE**

Robert Sheldon (ASCAP)

**49  CHORALE**

Chris M. Bernotas (ASCAP)

Slowly

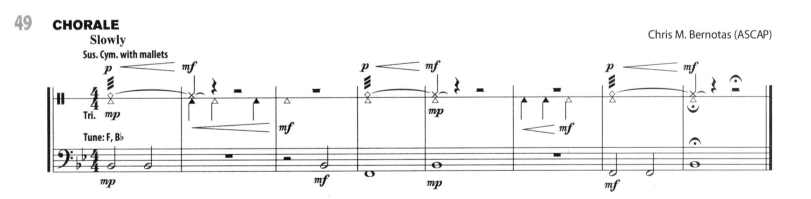

**50  CHORALE**

Roland Barrett (ASCAP)

# Concert G Minor

**51 LONG TONES**

**52 PASSING THE TONIC**

**53 EXPANDING INTERVALS: DIATONIC**

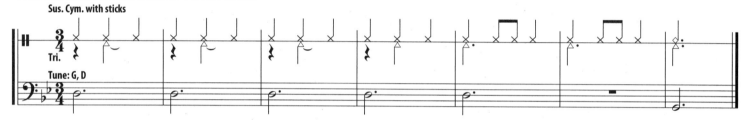

**54 INTERVAL BUILDER: DIATONIC INTERVALS**

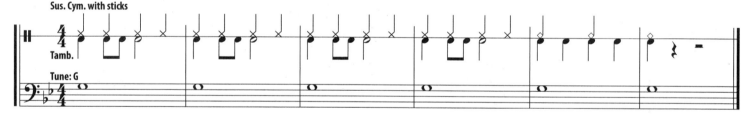

**55 CHORD BUILDER**

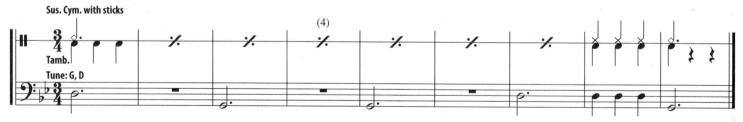

**56 DIATONIC HARMONY**

## 57 CHORALE: 5-NOTE SCALE

Chris M. Bernotas (ASCAP)

## 58 CHORALE: 8-NOTE SCALE (NATURAL MINOR)

Chris M. Bernotas (ASCAP)

## 59 CHORALE: 8-NOTE SCALE (HARMONIC MINOR)

Chris M. Bernotas (ASCAP)

## 60 CHORALE

Tyler S. Grant (ASCAP)

## 61 CHORALE

Rob Grice (ASCAP)

## 62 CHORALE

Robert Sheldon (ASCAP)

**63 CHORALE**

Moderately slow

Michael Story (ASCAP)

**64 CHORALE**

Randall D. Standridge (ASCAP)

**65 CHORALE**

Scott Watson (BMI)

**66 CHORALE**

Matt Conaway (ASCAP)

**67 CHORALE**

Roland Barrett (ASCAP)

**68 CHORALE**
John O'Reilly (ASCAP)

**69 CHORALE**
Chris M. Bernotas (ASCAP)

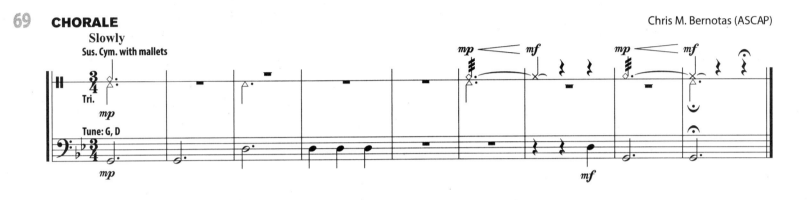

**70 CHORALE**
Ralph Ford (ASCAP)

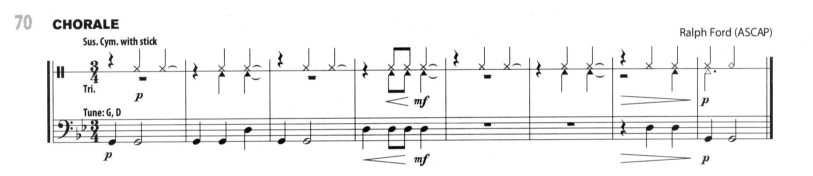

**71 CHORALE**
Tyler S. Grant (ASCAP)

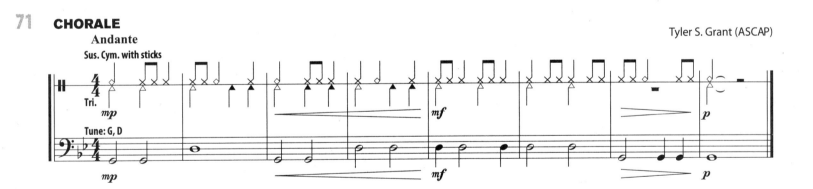

**72 CHORALE**
Jodie Blackshaw (ASCAP)

"She was determined to seek the truth, even if it meant losing everything."

scrape from crown to edge with coin

play 1st time only

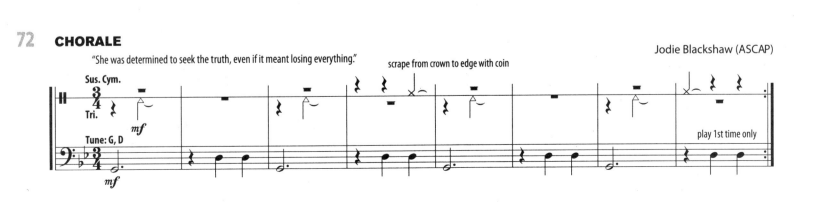

# Concert Eb Major

**73** **LONG TONES**

**74** **LONG TONES**

**75** **PASSING THE TONIC**

**76** **PASSING THE TONIC**

**77** **SCALE BUILDER**

**78** **SCALE BUILDER**

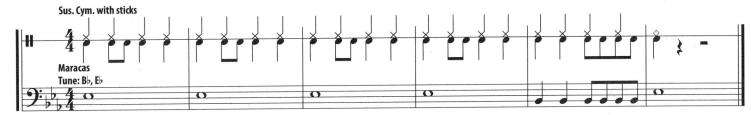
**79** **EXPANDING INTERVALS: DIATONIC**

**80** **EXPANDING INTERVALS: CHROMATIC**

**81** **INTERVAL BUILDER: DIATONIC INTERVALS**

**82** **INTERVAL BUILDER: PERFECT INTERVALS**

**83** **CHORD BUILDER**

**84** **CHORD BUILDER**

**85** **MOVING CHORD TONES**

**86** **DIATONIC HARMONY**

**87** **DIATONIC HARMONY**

**88** **RHYTHMIC SUBDIVISION**

**89** **5-NOTE SCALE**

**90** **CANON: 5-NOTE SCALE**

**91** **CANON: 6-NOTE SCALE**

17

**92  CANON: 8-NOTE SCALE**

**93  CHORALE: 5-NOTE SCALE**

Chris M. Bernotas (ASCAP)

**94  CHORALE: 5-NOTE SCALE**

Chris M. Bernotas (ASCAP)

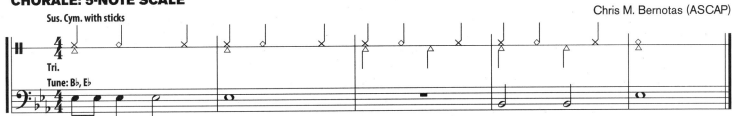

**95  CHORALE: 6-NOTE SCALE**

Chris M. Bernotas (ASCAP)

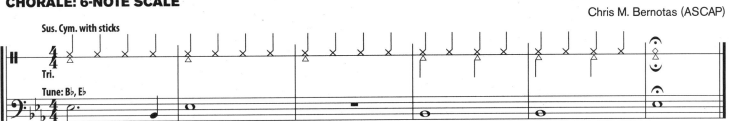

**96  CHORALE: 8-NOTE SCALE**

Chris M. Bernotas (ASCAP)

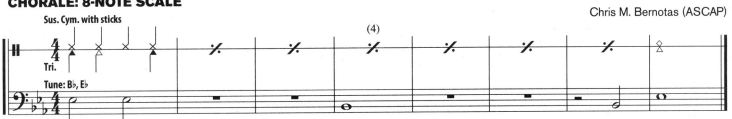

**97  CHORALE: 8-NOTE SCALE**

Chris M. Bernotas (ASCAP)

**98** **CHORALE**

Maestoso

Todd Stalter (ASCAP)

**99** **CHORALE**

Moderately slow

Michael Story (ASCAP)

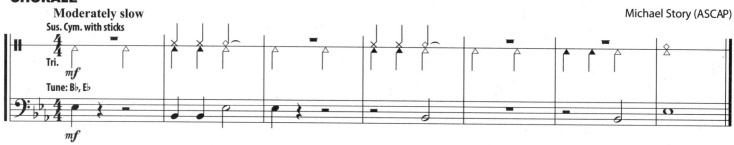

**100** **CHORALE**

Rob Grice (ASCAP)

**101** **CHORALE**

Gently

Matt Conaway (ASCAP)

**102** **CHORALE**

Moderato

John O'Reilly (ASCAP)

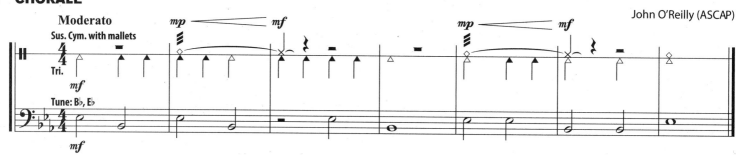

**103** **CHORALE**

Moderato

Scott Watson (BMI)

**104  CHORALE**

Roland Barrett (ASCAP)

**105  CHORALE**

Ralph Ford (ASCAP)

**106  CHORALE**

Rob Grice (ASCAP)

**107  CHORALE**

Tyler S. Grant (ASCAP)

**108  CHORALE**

Chris M. Bernotas (ASCAP)

**109  CHORALE**

Robert Sheldon (ASCAP)

**110  CHORALE**

Todd Stalter (ASCAP)

**111  CHORALE**

Jodie Blackshaw (ASCAP)

"In the mist there lurked a dark shadowy figure. Could it be?"

**112  CHORALE**

Matt Conaway (ASCAP)

**113  CHORALE**

Tyler S. Grant (ASCAP)

**114  CHORALE**

John O'Reilly (ASCAP)

**115  CHORALE**

Michael Story (ASCAP)

22

# Concert C Minor

**122 LONG TONES**

**123 PASSING THE TONIC**

**124 EXPANDNG INTERVALS: DIATONIC**

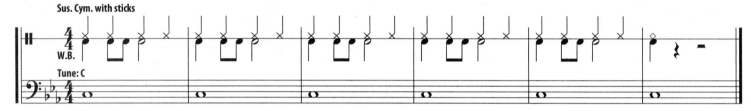

**125 INTERVAL BUILDER: DIATONIC INTERVALS**

**126 CHORD BUILDER**

**127 DIATONIC HARMONY**

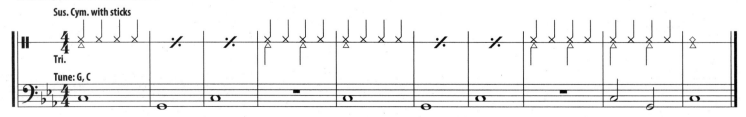

23

# 128 CHORALE: 5-NOTE SCALE

Chris M. Bernotas (ASCAP)

# 129 CHORALE: 8-NOTE SCALE (NATURAL MINOR)

Chris M. Bernotas (ASCAP)

# 130 CHORALE: 8-NOTE SCALE (HARMONIC MINOR)

Chris M. Bernotas (ASCAP)

# 131 CHORALE

Tyler S. Grant (ASCAP)

# 132 CHORALE

Rob Grice (ASCAP)

# 133 CHORALE

Ralph Ford (ASCAP)

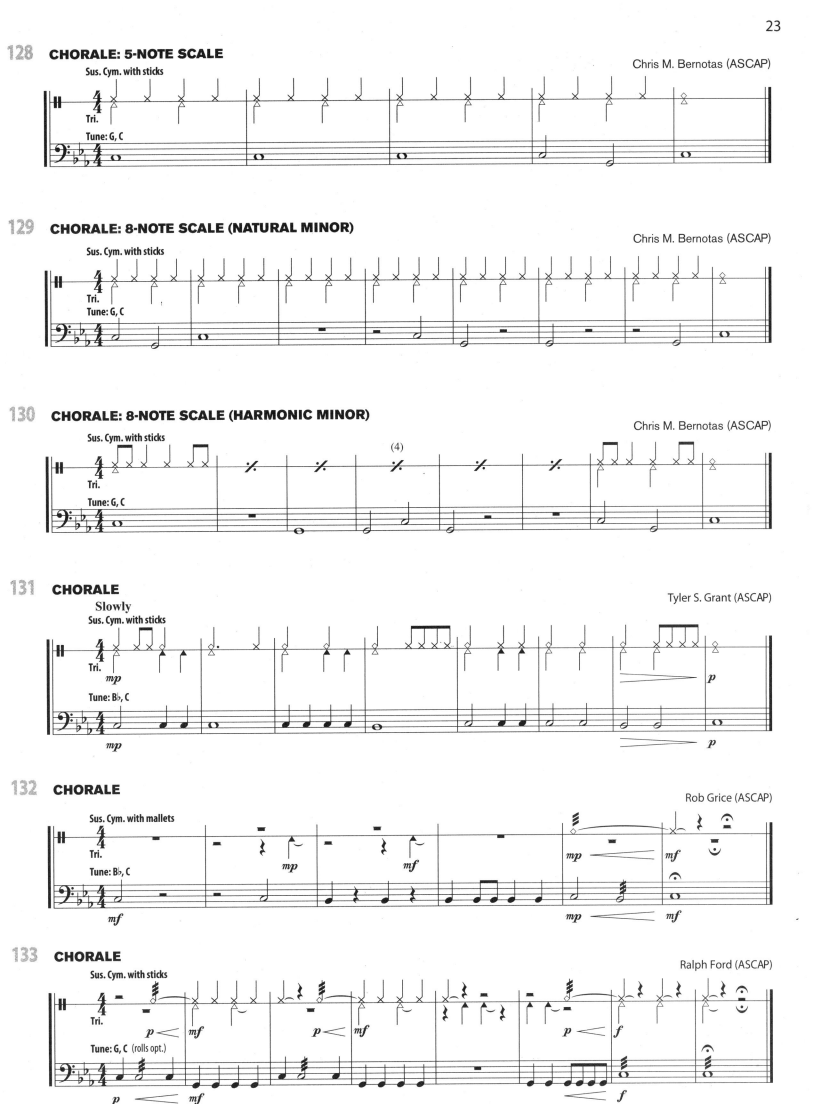

24

**134 CHORALE**

Robert Sheldon (ASCAP)

**135 CHORALE**

Michael Story (ASCAP)

**136 CHORALE**

Scott Watson (BMI)

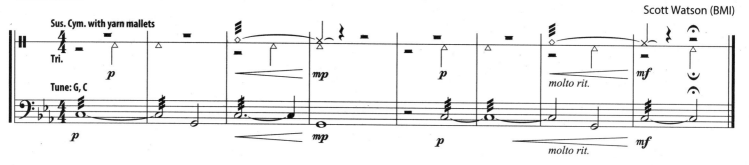

**137 CHORALE**

Matt Conaway (ASCAP)

**138 CHORALE**

Rob Grice (ASCAP)

## 139 CHORALE

Chris M. Bernotas (ASCAP)

## 140 CHORALE

Randall D. Standridge (ASCAP)

## 141 CHORALE

Jodie Blackshaw (ASCAP)

"Through the haze they glared at each other. He'd been waiting a long time for this."

## 142 CHORALE

Roland Barrett (ASCAP)

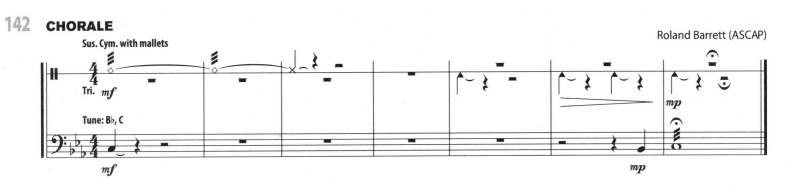

## 143 CHORALE

John O'Reilly (ASCAP)

# Concert F Major

**144  PASSING THE TONIC**

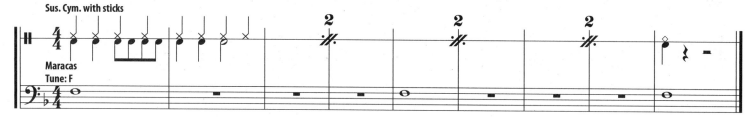

**145  EXPANDING INTERVALS: CHROMATIC**

**146  CHORD BUILDER**

**147  DIATONIC HARMONY**

**148  CHORALE: 6-NOTE SCALE**

Chris M. Bernotas (ASCAP)

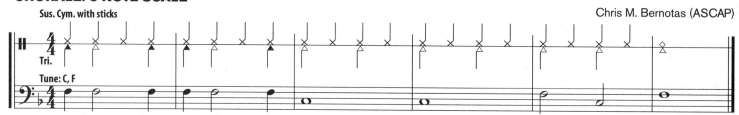

**149  CHORALE**

Rob Grice (ASCAP)

**150** CHORALE

Ralph Ford (ASCAP)

**151** CHORALE

Scott Watson (BMI)

**152** CHORALE

Randall D. Standridge (ASCAP)

**153** CHORALE

John O'Reilly (ASCAP)

**154** CHORALE

Roland Barrett (ASCAP)

**155** CHORALE

Adapted from Psalm 150, Claude Goudimel
Arranged by Todd Stalter (ASCAP)

# Concert D Minor

**156** **PASSING THE TONIC**

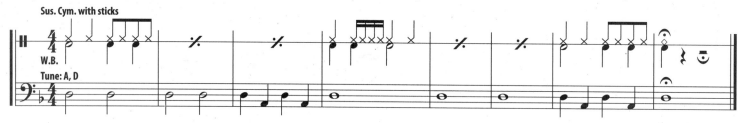

**157** **CHORD BUILDER**

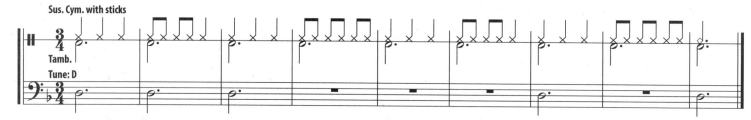

**158** **DIATONIC HARMONY**

**159** **CHORALE: 8-NOTE SCALE (HARMONIC MINOR)**

Chris M. Bernotas (ASCAP)

**160** **CHORALE**

Roland Barrett (ASCAP)

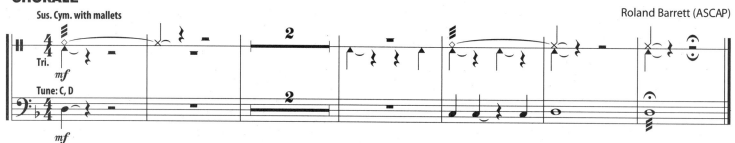

**161** **CHORALE**

Robert Sheldon (ASCAP)

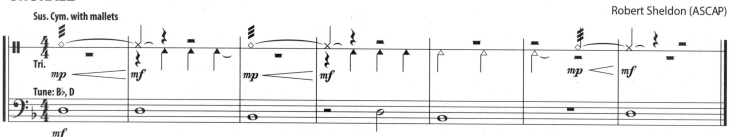

**162** **CHORALE**

Todd Stalter (ASCAP)

**163** **CHORALE**

Scott Watson (BMI)

**164** **CHORALE**

Michael Story (ASCAP)

**165** **CHORALE**

Ralph Ford (ASCAP)

**166** **CHORALE**

Tyler S. Grant (ASCAP)

**167** **CHORALE**

Jodie Blackshaw (ASCAP)

"In the darkness all she could hear was the sound of her beating heart. What had she done?"

# Timpani

## INSTRUMENT PLACEMENT & PLAYING POSITION

Timpani are usually positioned so the lowest drum is to your left. If using more than two drums, arrange them in a semi-circle with the pedals facing you.

Stand behind the drums with your feet comfortably spread for proper balance and weight distribution. Some players prefer to lean against a stool to help facilitate pedal changes and to bring the arm position down to a comfortable playing position.

## THE MALLET GRIP

The "German" grip, as opposed to the "French" grip, is often used by beginning players and is similar to the matched grip used for playing the snare drum. Let's review the matched grip:

A. First, extend your right hand as if you were going to shake hands with someone.

B. Place the mallet between your thumb and the first joint of your index finger, approximately ⅓ the way up from the end of the mallet.

C. Curve the other fingers around the shaft of the mallet.

D. Turn your hand over so your palm is facing towards the floor.

E. Repeat steps A–D with your left hand.

## TUNING

Most beginning students start off matching the pitch from an external source such as a pitch pipe or keyboard percussion instrument. It is important to listen for pitch relationships within the ensemble (soloist, chord, etc.) and to check your tuning periodically.

## STRIKING THE DRUM

Depending on the size of the drum, strike the head about 2 to 5 inches in from the bowl's edge making sure the heads of both mallets are side by side. To produce the best tone, the forearms should be relaxed and nearly parallel to the floor when the head is struck. Immediately following impact, the mallet should rebound without restriction.

## ROLLS

The timpani roll is one of the most characteristic sounds of the instrument and is produced by using rapidly alternating single strokes. Rolls are notated in the same manner as those for snare drum.

## MUFFLING/DAMPENING

In order to control the amount of sustain, it may be necessary to dampen/muffle the head. This can be accomplished by using the last two or three fingers of either hand to stop the vibration. Players will sometimes dampen a note simultaneously while striking another to avoid the mixture of the two sounds.

## CARE & MAINTENANCE

When not in use, heads should be covered with fiberboard discs and mallets should be kept in a stick bag or case. When moving the instrument, lift the drum from the struts rather than the counterhoop. When rolling or moving the drums over a threshold, make sure you lift the pedal mechanism from the floor.

# Accessory Percussion Instruments

## CRASH (HAND) CYMBALS

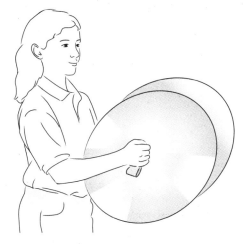

A. Start with a basic pair of sixteen- to eighteen-inch medium-weight cymbals.

B. Grasp the strap between the top of the first joint of the index finger and the flat, fleshy part of the thumb (close to the top of the bell). Do not put your hands through the loop of the straps.

### PLAYING THE CRASH CYMBALS

A. Hold the cymbals at approximately chest level.

B. For a right-handed player, keep the left cymbal stationary and strike the right cymbal against it with a glancing blow. The right cymbal should strike the left cymbal at an angle to avoid an air pocket. Once the crash has been executed, the cymbals should move apart so they can ring freely.

C. The distance between the cymbals will be wider for louder crashes and smaller for softer ones.

D. To muffle or choke the cymbals, draw them against your chest or forearms.

## THE SUSPENDED CYMBAL

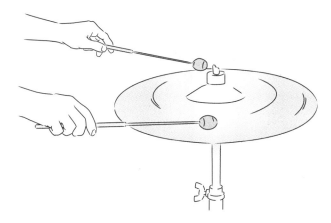

A suspended cymbal may be played with drumsticks or a variety of marimba and timpani mallets. Rhythmic passages are best articulated with snare drum sticks played near the edge.

### CARE AND MAINTENANCE

A. Fingerprints and dirt can be removed by using a solution of mild liquid detergent and warm water. Most cymbal manufactures also market specially formulated cymbal-cleaning products as well.

B. Never use steel wool, wire brushes or other abrasive cleansers.

## THE WOODBLOCK

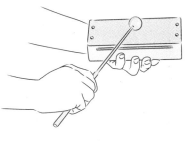

A. The woodblock may be played by holding it in the hand, mounted to a clamp (attached to a stand), or placed on a padded table. To produce the best tone, cup your hand to form a resonating chamber and strike the top center above the open slit. For fast, articulate passages, place the woodblock on a padded table and play it with two sticks or mallets.

B. It is most commonly played with medium-hard to hard rubber xylophone mallets. The tip or shoulder of a drumstick may also be used for more articulate passages.

## THE TAMBOURINE

A. Hold the tambourine in one hand with your thumb placed on the head and your fingers wrapped around the shell. It should be held at least chest high and at a slight angle to the floor.

B. For soft, rapid passages, place the tambourine on a horizontal, towel-covered music stand or padded table, and play it with the fingertips, sticks or mallets.

## THE TRIANGLE

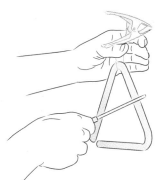

A The triangle is suspended from a triangle clip with a thin piece of nylon line. It can be held with the hand (at eye level), or attached to a music stand.

B. It is usually played with a steel beater and may be struck in a variety of spots, including the bottom or the side opposite the opening.